We are traveling through dark
at tremendous speeds.

We are traveling through dark at tremendous speeds.

We are traveling through dark
at tremendous speeds.

Sarah Sadie

We are traveling through dark
at tremendous speeds.

Sarah Sadie

Copyright © Sarah Sadie 2016

All rights reserved

ISBN: 978-1-943170-16-6

Cover and Interior Design: Jane L Carman
Typefaces: Garamond and Courier Prime

Published by: Lit Fest Press, Carman, 688 Knox Road 900 North, Gilson, Illinois 61436

There are no rules.
festivalwriter.org

You would see she exists

*For Reed, who knew to leave the princess water toys right where they were.*

*The roots of language are irrational and of a magical nature....Poetry wants to return to that ancient magic. Without fixed rules, it makes its way in a hesitant, daring way, as if moving in darkness.*
—Jorge Luis Borges
*from the* Prologue to The Self and the Other

*One never knows, do one.*
—Fats Waller

in defined space composed of small

# Contents

### Chapter One

Imagine a Mask of Feathers
I Am a Small Bird, Sir, But Brave
Seven Acorns Saved Too Long
Love in the Season of Great Horned Owls

### Chapter Two

Lullaby with Cobweb
U-Pick Strawberries
Love Does Call Us to the Things of This World
Folding the Clothes
The Rumor of Buttons, the Knowledge of Shirts
Really Seeing the Coffee Table
The Empathy Party

### Chapter Three

Riff on the Definition of Poem
Please Excuse Her Ignorance Re: the Pathetic Fallacy
Youth Was Armor Enough
Each Jar Tied with Bright Red Ribbon
Memories of Two Lights: Notes for a Quilt
Jingle Bells Bequeathed by an Uncle
No Title Here
Interior Monologue with Invited Guest
Purple Balloon

detail: apples, thread, car keys, what's for dinner Wednesday. Then again,

## Chapter Four

Song
Magnolias in Wisconsin
Love in the Season of Great Horned Owls
The Second Dream
Letter to My Daughter from Vernal Falls

## Chapter Five

The Girl the Gods Let Go
Byzantium at the Bus Stop, Byzantium at the Mall
Houdini's Key
Stretch Marks
Love in the Season of Great Horned Owls
Lullaby sans
Autobiographies

Acknowledgments

what is small? What is composed? Why does she feel the floor continually threatening to melt out from under her feet?

Chapter One:
We are traveling through dark at

Middle-aged, middle-class, middle-western. Flyover territory. The long
stretch through the pitted field. Potential comic interest. Unlikely
antonym of central. Closer to muddle. The soup, the swamp, the undefined.

*Some small, rabid, and very articulate animal lives in my throat.*

Sarah Sadie

## Imagine a Mask of Feathers

Oddly invisible, and without
the matching set of wings—
don't try to draw this at home
you'll only freeze a falsehood:
carnival gimmick, plastic
souvenir, flat with sequins and
the leaping eye shadow—

What we're after, you and I,
is the *feel*, the downy
whirr, soft tickle, that—
when you press in (press in)—keeps
sinking back. We want
the low trill, the pulse, the brush—
plunder.   pillow.

This is not, after all, some bright
exotic thing. Imagine the wren
or the owl. Imagine the dove,
caught. Imagine the fingers nestled,
*down. In.*

```
Where are we again? How did we get here? Where is the exit?
```

*We are traveling through dark at tremendous speeds.*

## I Am a Small Bird, Sir, But Brave

I am building me a new nest, a house out over the river,
of bits of stuffs, string, feathers, wrappers, junk  *junk junk*

It's a small house you're building, little bird.
                Two rooms only, sir, but quite enough
for all war starts in the bedroom, all business
in the kitchen. So the world spins  *whit whit*
Though it may be the opposite is true.

That it ends, rather than begins?

                Oh no, I never knew no end to either.
But it may be business in the bed, as I guess,
and war may lie with the knives and forks…

Most people are not happy. There's a bit for you.
A fine, a bitter bit. Most people are not—*too-whit, too-whoo.*

And what would make you happy, little bird?

The sweetest joy is motherhood. Another bit saved up
these pretty years but mark you
how it's lasted, oh, it's lasted.  *whit*
there's light to see by, though not
so much as you might want.

The deepest rivers can't be spoke,
nor would you have me say 'em.  *chirr*
Nor am I not the wren, sir, nor not the kingfisher.
But like, sir. Something like. A quick panic,
and there's truth for you.  *whit whit   junk junk junk*
The first time out's always a panic,
but I may at it, even so.

```
If she could move from thread and grocery lists to questions of destiny,
love, death—but life
```

### Seven Acorns Saved Too Long

These meant to mark a walk late last summer, our annual
only camping trip, my trotting daughter singing
through sun-spilled deciduous, my son on his scooter kicking ahead
and doubling back. *So fast, I go so fast.*
Below us a river wanders.

We followed it coming here, through a small town of tomato growers
lining their bucket gardens along the one road
running through, squeezed between the bluffs and river.
Oh long moon of rains, the earth squelches
and shifts by footsteps, and trees

profligate as parades toss us their small green bobbles.
The wobbly tumblers make me smile. I pocket another.
Seven in all, kept to track my return to that trail
this morning, as again the furnace clicks on with a hiss,
this winter of record snow.

Just two ways I know to slow time down. Hold it
in amber or weave it in rough green tapestries. Look. There we are,
still traipsing that soggy forest, overfed river below.
Truth's the moth at work on the corner, to say,
we broke camp early next day,

chased out by bugs, the muggy weather, the rain's return.
Dirty, streaked with woodsmoke and deet, we beat it home
and I was glad to be back.




interrupts in the opposite direction, insists in the shape of her daughter
wandering in wondering where her boots are,

*We are traveling through dark at tremendous speeds.*

> We leak our DNA
> all over the place. Some part of my ingrate heart
> threw itself away
> on that boarded-up main street driving through and rented
> a room in a closed-down town and lives there still. Did I think
> there was magic in these? Because they made me smile? Toss them all.
> The truth is nothing pretty or easy, but even
> truth will admit
>
> here comes my son wheeling back again, to ask if we saw,
> that time, how fast he was going.

`of the non-negotiable need to finish errands before the school bus arrives.`

Sarah Sadie

## Love in the Season of Great Horned Owls

*One—no two!*          —the kids exclaim—
*in our backyard!* We dig around
for binoculars and bird guides, turn
chairs to windows, curse the crows
mobbing our mornings and try to translate
the wild of owls into English,
the hours to feathers, learn how and where
to search for them, until our eyes
grow owl-shaped (finches forgotten)
until we can spot them: set deep back
in the spruce's branches, night hovering.
We learn if we can how to live
with taloned power perched in the willows.

In order for there to be a story, a man has to pass by. So she catches a glimpse and falls, fatefully. (Some things are predictable.) So she marries him and bears a child. So Undine gains a soul and loses her immortality. That's what they tell us.

*I created a space for her to emerge, and then she created me.*

Chapter Two:
We are traveling through

At the time it must seem the right choice.

*Who you tell the story to shapes the story.*

Sarah Sadie

## Lullaby with Cobweb

Unhook, unhook, and lock the door
I do not live here any more

All the tethers that bound me fast
I've loosed and freed myself at last

All the *pretty* all the *nice*
I've turned myself to night and ice

I've turned myself to hiss and stare
to owl, naiad, bald aware

Unhook, unhook, and lock the door
I do not live here any more

What are those boots? We are delivered to comedy. "Mrs. B. gave up trying
to fathom

*We are traveling through dark at tremendous speeds.*

## U-Pick Strawberries

### 1.

We drove to U-pick strawberries each year,
to a small-town farm where breezes off the ocean
zephyred through the long-striped fields of fruit
and artichokes. Our kids
just babies, everything still potential and ripe
berries so hay-sweet, the only answer
we could dream was *yes*.

That town was more or less one street, made up
of cottages for migrant labor, antique
emporiums, a local grocery store
in an old barn, sea sand blown in, gritty
underfoot. Twice a day, they baked
an artichoke bread on-site. People would loiter
in the aisles, absently handling toothpaste
or lemons, waiting for the cart to roll out
with all those steaming loaves, wrapped in brown paper.
We'd drive out to the beach, flats in the back,
warm bread in hand, find a table or
a driftwood log and tear that tender loaf
and eat it then and there and that was dinner.
Bread that good, we thought it was enough.

That was where the Pescadero emptied
into Half Moon Bay, and that was where we'd head,
up river from the surf to quieter water.
And if you wanted, they grew blackberries too,
and if you wanted, you could get a loaf
without the artichokes, and if you wanted
and who doesn't, sometimes.

the ways of fate and fortune and focused instead on the refrigerator's
innards, which had been ripening noticeably since Tuesday."

2.
Twice I went alone. The last time out
I had both kids, my infant daughter strapped
in carrier, trying to nap, and—
a friend, from out of state.

I didn't feel yet what
I wanted, what it was would happen to us—not
that day, but in the days to come—and then
it was time to go and where,
where was my son's blue cup? Buried and lost
in a toddler's game. And even
in that minute, that windy, too-cold day,
with crabby infant, sobbing toddler, setting
sun and friendship yet untested, I knew
that it's right to lose things, to return home
not quite whole, and knowing it.


3.
All this came back to me today, seeing
the first of the strawberries up from Mexico,
the blessing of trucked fruit arrived in Middleton,
sour, a little tough, and a far cry from that easy yes.
And that explains my gladness at our move, more or less.

---

Where I live the streets are designed to curl and confuse. There are no easy intersections and the landscape begins to wild. I post links to my poems online and stick them into occasional small magazines.

*We are traveling through dark at tremendous speeds.*

## Love Does Call Us to the Things of This World

This morning love opened the bedroom door
to tell me my son spilled candlewax on the carpet
and do I know how to get that out?
Yes, love, I do. And so with the iron, and so
with the newspaper, day not yet broken.
But it's a slow job and love needs breakfast
before heading to the busstop. I pause in my labor
for scrambled eggs, hot chocolate, the hurried comb
through the hair, protestations of pain, "Mo-o-om!"
Oh, love enters the bus crying, and this afternoon
will skip all the way home. Love is patient with me:
the wax is still there, mild and mossy green, waiting
when I return.

I am my father's daughter. The truest love
is an argument, holding on hard and pulling against.
So it's love, when I read the line about rosy hands
and steam, and let there be nothing but laundry, it's love
that cries out, *This is a great poem, but what—but what—
Nothing but laundry! What a sentence! A sentencing!*
And it's love, that says to the man in that poem,
as he rises from bed to tell his wife or his mother to bring in
the clothes from the line, oh then love responds, saying,
*Honey, never you mind. Those clothes will dry in their own time.
The bacon is sizzling, the coffee is hot.* And I'm the one, after all,
who knows which shirt belongs to the lover, which to the thief,
who knows how to fold them all, and lay them
away, dark in the bed of the drawer.

Bread crumbs.

Sarah Sadie

## Folding the Clothes

Even the most capacious bath towels fold
into squares, and the wash cloths fold
into smaller squares. Pants meet themselves

and quiet down nicely. Underwear
resigns itself, socks domesticate, and the shirts,
well, the shirts get wrinkled.

They'll have plenty of time to relax
dreaming through hours a rumor of buttons.
Which is not to say shirts meditate, but

there's almost a Zen to the job, if that weren't so trendy.
Almost the little sand garden with its rake
and its rock.
                                      Its imagined snake.

```
My transports an odyssey and my husband's accord, they may masquerade as
tame, but my tenor shatters glass, I hope.
```

*We are traveling through dark at tremendous speeds.*

## The Rumors of Buttons, the Knowledge of Shirts

The shirts listened, curious and pained,
as their buttons fumbled, but never quite explained
the ecstasy of thumbs, sweet in and out,
how lonely to gape separate.

They knew a gleam at lonely, but otherwise—
no. They did not understand their buttons' sighs.
*Armpits*, thought the shirts. *Elbows*, whispered they,
and that pale nightmare, *fray*.

```
Somewhere along about halfway, she becomes nocturnal. Night waits all day,
just at the roots, cool around the ankles. At evening, it seeps up, up
until she is submerged in that new element, those hours
```

## Really Seeing the Coffee Table

For all it took more than four months to arrive,
it does look good. He thinks the wood's too dark,
it doesn't match. But I prefer it. He tells how
he had to maintain the glass top's balance, level,
even as he matched and bolted corners
from underneath. *The directions must have assumed
zero gravity*, he jokes. But I'm not listening,

distracted by an article, or email, or the kids,
or even not distracted, just long married.

Later, drifting in or out of sleep,
I see him clearly, alone with the task he has
assigned himself, the awkward, slidey weight of it,
so hard to hold, hold up, and still fix all
in place. And how do we decipher these
instructions, always wordless, and the drill's
power cord just a bit too short?

```
when her house fills with breathing of sleepers. Boundaries blur in the
dark, time bends non-linear, and shapes may shift. Night is when she
```

*We are traveling through dark at tremendous speeds.*

### The Empathy Party

My son barred me from the empathy party
his fifth grade classroom hosted. In our
evolving dance there are
so many events I'm not invited to, moments
I'm too intimate to share.

Later, he tells me he thought the snacks sucked,
crackers and carrot sticks, and
there was too much applause and why
did the visiting parents get to eat before the kids,
who after all did all the work?

I try to explain about guests and hosts, care
and respect but he will have none of it.
His future parties will be free for alls, he promises,
everyone digging in, no deference paid
to custom, age, grace nor gratitude.

So I switch tracks. *What were the empathy stories your class shared?*
Someone didn't kill a spider by their bed.
Someone and her brother named the motherless
rabbit kits in their back yard. Someone
let someone else score a soccer goal.

*And you, what was your story?*

*There was a kid being mean to me, so I
called him a Baloney, and when he told me
that hurt his feelings, I stopped.*

She collects I's: Intimacy, Intensity and Immediacy. Motherhood adds two more: Interruption and Insistence.

*It's not the blank page that scares me, it's the blank behind the page.*

*The recipe to make paper:*
*1. Tear up the old paper.*

Chapter Three:
We are

She's more than half way to spider.

Sarah Sadie

## Riff on the Definition of Poem

A book is a basket of deaths. Small ones.
A web with no spider (hide
her), this is the secret dilation,
the interior shore, a little
lagniappe, something more,
a dance for the sake of dancing.

Verse. Reverse. Press in, be pressed
upon and disappear. Address,
redress and put your clothes on, honey.
Embrace arrest. Treat and retreat. Flight
does not equal resist. This is

the walled garden, the invitation,
an intimate penetration.
Let's not lie or cover over.
It's sexy as hell, what's going on.

How can she paint a self-portrait. How can she paint anything but. I'm
changing my name, she tells her husband. What's changed? he asks.

*We are traveling through dark at tremendous speeds.*

## Please Excuse Her Ignorance Re: the Pathetic Fallacy

It was all too much, we knew. We blushed
at how storm-riddled the weather was
that stretch, and how she wasn't thinking
about the weather, trading reds
for raisins to paint her mouth a crooked
on, ready to dishevel.

The season, the season, we hissed, think, *think*—
but climate change or what you will,
those over-the-top thunderheads
came on, and on, no less than five
tornadoes touching down. All
her instruments gone blunt, crazy,

needles dialing south. The ground
stayed soft, waterlogged.
We stayed indoors, turned on the air,
as, through summer steam and mist, she rose,
her strangely words fluting wrong but kissable,
her thighs so heavy she could hardly walk.

```
I'm not going to smile for the camera.
```

Sarah Sadie

## Youth Was Armor Enough

Remember when we pitched our tents,
young as we were, above Superior's gray shore,
and discovered there a steep path to the back
we hadn't seen before? Down it led us,
to a private cove, protected. From that vantage,
the whole lake could have been ours—
imagine the luck!—and no flies.

The water calm and the afternoon warm,
we stripped off our packs and all we'd worn
or carried, to wade into that ancient element
wearing nothing but youth.

Any blessing carries its shadow, sometimes for years,
folded like the wings of a bat at noon.
How grateful I am, friends, for that shared memory,
now that I have reached another interior shore,
this time alone, and again to strip down,
whatever I thought I could carry in, again
to enter the still and waiting waters.

How do you define invisible? We don't need myth to tell us that

*We are traveling through dark at tremendous speeds.*

## Each Jar Tied with Bright Red Ribbon

Why, turning, does my life
small itself so readily, restricting
its contours to the idea of making
homemade peanut butter with my daughter,

which leads my son to declare he will not
make anything for anybody, that he
dislikes Christmas in general and won't
even eat the cookies this year, in protest.

Meanwhile I wonder if daughter rhymes
with peanut butter, once again my attention
riveted to the fleeting fascinations of my children:
the color wheel, weather, dinosaurs.

These become my metaphors but before
I've written anything they've moved on
to Greek myth, carnation pink.
Any of these worth an epic, a large canvas,

and I see how I could fit a few
naked women around the edges,
but my mind trends to handwork, the dropped
stitch no one else will notice.

as she, now mortal, begins to age, things change. Some things are
predictable. Curses. Betrayals. None of the ancient bards writes down what
happens to Undine after this.

Sarah Sadie

## Memories of Two Lights: Notes for a Quilt

Two large panels for the lighthouses, set off-center,
then scatter the smaller nine-patch blocks, *Rosa
Rugosa* blown wide open, light-and-sea-kissed, salted
sweet and simple on the diagonal. All of us cousins—

somewhere I'll have to work in the blue of the sky.
I remember it blue, although I also remember
the repeating blare of the two horns out of the fog,
and a baby—your son—crying at the noise.

A grit of wind and rock and what sand there was,
all in your palette of brown and tan, and there
down in the corner, the picnic tables everyone
ranged about. A quilt could never convey

the taste of those sandwiches—Italians, you called them,
each wrapped and taped in grease-stained newspaper,
peppers and pickles and seasoned oil-soaked rolls,
the tang and brine of onions, olives, the brine

of the salt Atlantic unrolling before us in waves and bolts,
measured but never cut. All of us cousins—
nine-patch scattered and skewed on the diagonal
across the whole surface, pieced into the borders even.

Some follow him a little way down the path.

*We are traveling through dark at tremendous speeds.*

## Jingle Bells Bequeathed by an Uncle

Big as a child's fist, riveted
to thick leather at regular intervals,
unwieldy as the cold solstice earth,
theirs no aeolian song set off
by a breeze, no giggle that batman
smells and robin laid his egg:
it takes real muscle, not
some hoked-up gadget belt,
to set these bells to ringing.

Here in my well-lit, twenty-first century
house, we have no horses.
We hang the bells on the banister and if
we want them to ring, we do it ourselves,
which the kids do, repeatedly, laughing,
wearing the finish off the wood.

And when they do, it's nothing close
to the tiny, tinny clatter we know
from preschool circle time.
Like watersound, this bellflow music tumbles us
into Currier & Ives nostalgia for a never was,
if I'm not careful, all of us nestled
with other happy carolers, the runners hushed
and swift over the sparked snow, horses
high-stepping, the clear night filled
with snatches of song and laughter, house
to house all lit from within and other parties waving...
*Hello, hello! Merry Christmas...*

Poetry shares its five eyes, nonlinearity and focus on the specific with the old tales, the tales we consign to children. In these stories usual hierarchies of relevance tumble. The very small (a crust of bread, a mouse, a golden needle or simple handkerchief) suddenly proves crucial to the adventure's success.

Sarah Sadie

> No. Scrap all that as junk,
> microwave the apple cider and splash
> the whiskey in to toast the man. Then toast
> the echoes of that imagined caroling party, off into the dark—
>
> *Farewell, farewell, goodbye* and where are we off to next –
> That part is real enough.

Any larger question becomes distraction.

*We are traveling through dark at tremendous speeds.*

## No Title Here

Pain continued planet-wide against
that sunrise, particular

(you on your bed of tears) as needles
as clouds overhead immolated in reds,

pinks, marbled gold—two-minute gift
and warning of storm.

Once, one year in a fairy tale together.
Now the fairy ending—path

of Technicolor cloud (oh walk proud
prince) all the way to the gold

and burning heart.

But that was in the middle
of your long dying, not at the end

and now that I've managed
to write it down you're dead.

Drug companies want us to believe eight hours of unbroken sleep each night is normal. Nothing could be further from truth.

## Interior Monologue with Invited Guest

Aren't we lucky
it's not the stunned and empty field
I warned you to expect? No,
here's croquet, and college students,
and wine in plastic cups for faculty.
It's a picnic, darling, and I'd guess
it's August, and it will be August
for years. Aren't we lucky
it's such a social space, with noise
of conversation, noise of laughter.
Half the guests are ghosts and aren't we
lucky they agreed to come,
unpacked from memory into this
backyard of my childhood,
one of so many. How random. How
delightful. How did I pull it off?

Aren't you amused? Aren't
we lucky you could make it too,
the only stranger, the only real
invisible, in time to taste
the apples pressed to cider in the shed.

In time to see this view
through a long ago window.
Isn't it delicious, apples, plums, the potluck
slaws and salads, students, croquet,
the cold bad wine oh maybe
I conjure you only to say goodbye.
Goodbye, bad doll, sad substitute.
And if I repeat the act,
one hundred times, one hundred scenes,
will I believe it? Tell me, will I?

```
The narrative trickles off into question marks and the audience grows
bored, demands to hear about some other naked nymph. And she
```

*We are traveling through dark at tremendous speeds.*

## Purple Balloon

Forsaken on the guest bathroom's closet floor,
scuttled behind a broken door, it's been there—
what, a year?—a little shrunken but still round,
it has attained some gaseous equilibrium,
now drifts and breathes quietly, attuned
to the friendly dust and spiders of my basement.

We're tired of you, balloon. Please go away.
Just fizzle out. Release your remnant helium,
so we don't have to get the scissors. You've lost
your wonder, no longer hovering overhead,
no longer lifting, lofting when we bat at you.
We know not what to do with old balloons.

Years back, my husband stomped one and our son,
a toddler then, burst into tears. "A head,"
I said. "He must think it's a head—stop.
Stop!" We froze, appalled and guilty. What
did I know? I was only grabbing at some
guessed-at glimmer, hoping.

It turned out, never one to see imaginary friends,
he was only crying (likely) at the noise,
which was sudden, loud, and to him, inexplicable.

faces away from us.

*2. Mix with water.*

*3. Create new from the slurry. It is the same with the Self.*

Chapter Four:
We

Half of each week, my husband works in another part of the state. To
avoid a tedious daily commute, we bought a small, one-bedroom apartment
in that other town. Occasionally we drive the children over for a vacation
weekend.

*Find your spine and insist upon it.*

Sarah Sadie

## Song

Where knots of water lilies dangle
and watergrass and willow mingle

burble of carp an ancient laughter
up from the muck of the noontime shadows

this the riddle stuck in my throat
to worry the tangle of bed and heart

what do you think the woman finds
who dares the deep where moonlight bends?

what do you think that woman discovers
who sets down her shields where the water shivers?

as wild and green as Grendel's sister
the shadows at noon, the dark still water

The kids sleep on couch and floor but there's an indoor swimming pool and ping-pong and they love it.

*We are traveling through dark at tremendous speeds.*

## Magnolias in Wisconsin

No bigger than
a man, crabbed and flowering the briefest span

of days each spring, a week at most. The petals stark-
soft as milk against the still bare branches' rough-cragged bark.

Too quick, the blown
petals wet brown

and shriveled over the cooling grass,
a frayed and fraying lace.

Tonight, as I clean and ready for the journey home, I leave my daughter's three princess water toys in the bathtub for my husband to find next week, when he will see them as mess, detritus from a vacation that I overlooked, more proof of my careless housekeeping.

## Love in the Season of Great Horned Owls

One morning in still crepuscular light,
we see the male owl feed his mate
in silhouette against the dawn.
Their shadows merge and separate
as they bend.

Such tenderness I haven't seen
in a long time, though just last week
my husband said *I want to cook
for you, for Valentine's*. He does.
But he forgets

he asked me to choose the recipe,
procure ingredients. He makes
the wrong thing, and I am miffed.
A half-assed botchup of a gift
and I've drunk too much.

He looks at me *I'm trying here.*
*Well so am I*, I don't reply,
hassled by kids, by phone calls, by
the requirements of sunlight. We've both
messed up. Married

love is muscled and damn big, but hard
to spot, even with binoculars.

```
He'll sigh, audibly or not, and pick them up out of the bath, put them
away somewhere he won't see them until his daughter visits again.
```

*We are traveling through dark at tremendous speeds.*

## The Second Dream

In the second dream, gravity worked, but only
just. I swayed over the side of the bed as my legs
stretched languorously toward the ceiling fan,
my arms arced down, my hair cascading to the floor
because that is what hair does and that

is how you made me feel last night: elegant,
upside down, and half wobbly helium.
Of course I woke up. Gravity is inarguable
and my abs are not so toned.
Still, such a lovely sensation, I thought,

exactly like driving too fast over hills in the dark.
If I could just—in my cotton jammies,
my handknit socks, inching myself backwards
off the bed, hands and head to the floor, and then
one leg vaguely waving into air, if I could just

get the other—up—
and I burst out laughing
at my impossible, implausible self.
My husband ran in at the noise. *What*—he stopped,
staring at me, there. *What are you doing?*

*Nothing*, I said—and unbelievably, I didn't fall,
as I righted myself on the bed, straightened my shirt—
*It was a dream I had. It was*—I shook my head,
still laughing, and went off to assemble the day
into rhyme and eggs.

```
I leave them there anyway, emissaries.
```

Sarah Sadie

## Letter to My Daughter from Vernal Falls
*Yosemite*

Maybe it takes a mountain, and all its rock
refusals, to prove water's dizz and craze,
deepest capacities for plunge.

These mountains are too big, too unmoving.
They interrupt the sky, constrain the sun
to fall in narrow angles, slant steeply

across the tall tall trees which also do not move.
Your father laughs at this, but my eyes, raised
in a region of wind and light and

gossamer small ceaseless variation, grow
restless. Daughter, I have fallen
past floor a time or two.

I wish no less for you, in your forward movements.
But this morning, before anyone else stirs,
I'll add a postscript, because amid

the plash and roil, pool and burble, fish, mottled
dark against the stones and sand, swim low
nosing the rocks, resisting

the convincing element. It means something, this lithe
and muscled insistence I had to fight to learn.
The journey can't be rushed.

Sometimes it's right to resist the flow, the go go go.
Say that we took our time arriving. We turned,
swam across our own current

when we wanted. As we needed.

```
Belle sighing, Girls grow up.
Cinderella nods, tired. Even a queen grows restless.
```

*Toss out your compasses, clocks, maps. They will not work.*

Chapter Five

And Ariel, facedown, repeats *We were here. We were here.*

*Why does no one write of the courage it takes to search out moments to be happy?*

Sarah Sadie

## The Girl the Gods Let Go

One by one, I saw you, sisters, plucked,
picked out for flashing eyes or ankles,
the thick coils of your hair.
The gods delighted and away you went,
leaving me all those centuries ago.
I arrived each time alone at the riverbed.
Waiting, I practiced my sighs of alarm, gasps of delight,
I trailed my fingers through the water
just so, and sent fleet glances, right
then left, over my shoulders, and…nothing.
No one came. I was not pursued.
It proved a strange aerobics.

So I delivered myself at last to minivans
and pool parties you never dreamt.
Four kids and a successful spouse, a dog,
and all was well, more or less, until
I found my golden corset in the closet,
long buried, and, curious, I tried it on.
It hardly fit. Squashed to overflowing,
ablaze and breathless with memories and armor,
my knife sheathed at my hip, still sharp, but useless
and now needlessly ornate. And then my husband came in
*What the heck is that get up?*
*Nothing—*
*never mind—just help me take it off.*

```
Already she questions and crosses out her first sentences.
```

*We are traveling through dark at tremendous speeds.*

> I wept that night, missing you, missing
> the eyes of wild deer in the dark. But now,
> at last, a someone comes, cold, blank, to my bed.
> I wake to lead-colored bruises. Surrounded by shades
> of *if* and *never*, how could it be other?
> I did not have your graces, sisters, only
> clumsy passion and long memory,
> paltry gifts. But I have forged myself
> within twinned fires of regret and deep
> resentment. There are, still, those cold
> gods we never name. They need my heat.
> They gorge themselves on all my melting tears
> and nurse to strength, drinking my bitter milk.

```
The language baffles her into essays of erasure, circular palimpsests.
Spider webs
```

Sarah Sadie

## Byzantium at the Bus Stop, Byzantium at the Mall

Byzantium is no mythy place. I live here.
Yellowjackets turn aggressive
and bumblebees bump insistently into asters.
The ditches outside town fill to flood with goldenrod,
flame-shaped heads nodding in wind,
and soybeans sweep gold, wave
upon wave, fields emanating light until
the trees catch: honeylocust, then ash, and finally
the thrashing willows turn to yellow straw.
We're smack dab in glittering Byzantium,
a long stretch through a pitted field
as chirruping children board the bus
and marriages break up, because or in spite of us.

What shall we do?
Head tra-la to the mall for back-to-school sales,
to find damned Byzantium again
as every display demonstrates perfection,
all the arrows flashing You Are Here.
Not young nor old, but weathering
the stretch that no one talks about, for fear—
and yellow is very in this year.
Imagined ecstasy of vision, this prerecorded siren's song,
dizzy parade of music video and windowed mannequin,
they urge: even you may essay timelessness.
Here in Byzantium we find Byzantium's trace:
Victoria's Secret models with Theodora's face.

re-vision, re-phrase, spiral out and back in.

*We are traveling through dark at tremendous speeds.*

      Those bowls of light were always a thin broth,
   though for years I held up only happy endings (try this one on)
       doing my best to ignore peripheral movement, feral
             whispers of the undergrowth. No more.
            I sing down time and all the ravages,
             a wild watering, embrace the mud
             Byzantium was built upon, eternal
                 slurry that was always there.
              We fracture, fragment, patch it up
       and catch what light we can these flawed, mosaic days.
           Whatever's frozen, ageless, perfect I discard
                to build anew, shard by razor shard.

Language has not been invented.

Sarah Sadie

## Houdini's Key

The key
to freedom
in the kiss of
a wife (who would
think) this muscular
spectacular and mess
of flimdoodle all rolled
into one, handcuffed and
photographed, handcuffed
and photographed, over and
over like a local tough except this one
kept escaping underwater, in a box,
upsidedown, off a bridge: a Jewish
kid from Appleton turned into
(he'd say) the only superhero
who was ever real but
think what it meant
for—think what
it asked of
—her.

The five eyes of poetry stare me down. And so I try again.

*We are traveling through dark at tremendous speeds.*

## Stretch Marks

Once, when we were in a hard stretch,
my husband wrote me a note that said
*I can't imagine thinking your body*
*is sexy, in twenty years.*

It wasn't what he meant.
What was implied—he told me later—
was that although he couldn't
imagine it, he knew he would,
because now, twenty years already in,
he did, and at age nineteen
he couldn't have imagined that.

Love is what's between the lines.
We stopped writing notes.

What could be less sexy than
a woman writing down plain truth
about her body and her marriage?
This body is stretchmarked
from my shoulders to my knees,
as though a thousand pearl-eyed fish
shivered kisses as I surfaced
through time's suck and whinge.
Rucks and pockets and sprouted hair,
brought on by pregnancies and arguments
and weird hormonal shifts, now my skin
looks like the skin of a lake
when a chilly breeze ripples across.

Or skin of ocean.
(I have come to believe
life and love are questions of dilation.)
Against the shiny minor goddesses
I set moles, gray hair,
and crows feet, signs of good humor,
of pain endured and pain's release.
Odysseus returns, and realizes it doesn't
matter so much, what Penelope was doing
in the meantime. True minds again met,
their bed still a tree, and hadn't he
had his adventures too?

*We are traveling through dark at tremendous speeds.*

## Love in the Season of Great Horned Owls

Two babies perch side by side, blinking fuzzily.
In threes and fours, converted pilgrims bring
cameras and children, pick their way
through our yard to the sighting area.

The gods have need of us, yet.
My husband digs a garden, creates
a path of paving stones, and sets a bench.
And maybe the spell is larger than the owls,

for surely they don't care about our bleeding hearts,
astilbe, violets. Our garden collaborates
with something—what? Or is it only
with the neighbors and our neighborhood?

Each dusk we dot the yard in human constellations
and visit together, having been visited.

```
(Intuitive. Internal. Two more for your basket, dearie.)
```

Sarah Sadie

## Lullaby sans

Doppelganger, shadow, mask
the question you're afraid to ask

the hollow held in any ring
the song that you will never sing

the children you will never have
Grendel's sister, Sarah's hove

broken clock and scrying bowl
shadow of the great horned owl

and when at dusk the owl flies
I am its absence in the trees

*We are traveling through dark at tremendous speeds.*

## Autobiographies

The dark river unloosed.
The bright-eyed bird sought rest
in pine trees full of a broken clock
music of grackles, ditches full
of the chonk-a-ree of redwings.
It's a birdy world, a pratfall
of lost, pit of resist, as rinky-tink
meets honky-tonk, minister
meets medicine show meets last
night in the eyes and tempest
tossed. Comical and sad,
that glottal halt, salt water
taffy and the smell of lilac.
Listen. You can't go back.
Fallen and falling like a waterfall,
the music that cracks
the sturdy little egg of the world.

*We are far beyond nouns.*

# Acknowledgments

Some of these poems have appeared or are forthcoming in journals, magazines, and anthologies, sometimes in different versions, or with different titles (and under different names). Gratitude to the editors of all these publications for their dedication and service, time and energy.

*Adanna*: "The Second Dream"
*Junoesq*: "U-Pick Strawberries"
*Literary Mama*: "Each Jar Tied with Bright Red Ribbon"
*Mom Egg Review*: "Really Seeing the Coffee Table"
*Off the Coast*: "Love in the Season of Great Horned Owls" (2) and (3); "Please Excuse Her Ignorance Re: the Pathetic Fallacy"
*Quill and Parchment*: "Youth Was Armor Enough"
*Rose Red Review*: "Imagine a Mask of Feathers"; "The Girl the Gods Let Go"; "The Rumors of Buttons, the Knowledge of Shirts"
*String Poet*: "Magnolias in Wisconsin"
*Valparaiso Poetry Review*: "Folding the Clothes"
*Wisconsin People and Ideas*: "Memories of Two Lights"
*Wisconsin Poets' Calendar 2015*: "Riff on the Definition of Poem"
*Your Daily Poem*: "Jingle Bells Bequeathed by an Uncle"


"Houdini's Key" was part of a collaboration with Madison Museum of Contemporary Art, and was included in a published portfolio, limited edition.

"You Would See She Exists" (the river of text running and pooling and spilling across the floor of these pages) originally appeared in a different version in Vox-Mom, the online blog of the *Mom Egg Review*.

"I Am A Small Bird Sir, But Brave" appeared on Woodland Pattern's blog in April 2015.

*We are traveling through dark at tremendous speeds.*




The gifts of space, time, and the companionship of fellow poets cannot be overestimated. The original inspiration for this book's shape began a number of years ago at a Poet Camp retreat organized by Bruce Dethlefsen. Another fellow poet, Chuck Rybak, saw a version of this manuscript in infancy and was good enough not to laugh. Margaret Rozga, Norma Gay Prewett, Martha Kaplan, Lisa Vihos all added their insightful comments and encouragement along the way. Wendy Vardaman deserves a special shoutout for years of mutual poetic adventure, creative camaraderie, and countless rich conversations. Thank you and love to all my community of Wisconsin poets. I am lucky my circles stretch beyond the borders of our state, but there is a special place in my heart for my local writing fam.

Jane L. Carman and Lit Fest Press accepted a manuscript of loosely associated poems, impulses and fragments, and worked patiently with me for many months. There is much courage and creativity at the micro press level. The debt is mine.

This book would not have happened at all without the support of my family, most especially Reed, who withstands and stands with, and has proved himself game for most adventures.

Now it belongs to you, reader.

Once upon a time, there lived

We are traveling through dark
at tremendous speeds.

www.ingramcontent.com/pod-product-compliance
Lightning Source LLC
Chambersburg PA
CBHW051704090426
42736CB00013B/2539